DECISIONS
A Young Man's Guide to Avoiding
The
TRAPS

Written by

Patrick L. Phillips, MSW

DECISIONS: A Young Man's Guide to Avoiding
The
TRAPS

Copyright © 2014 by Patrick L. Phillips, MSW

MrPhillipsTheChangeAgent@gmail.com
info@mrphillipsthechangeagent.com

ISBN-10: 0989373916
ISBN-13: 978-0-9893739-1-3
Library of Congress Control Number 2014906241
Published by: Educational Empowerment Group, LLC

First Edition

Editing: MNG
Book Cover Design: Ms. Maurel Denge
Graphic Design: Creative Notions Design Group

DEDICATION

I would like to dedicate this book to my mother, Robbie Mitchell, for making the sacrifices as a single parent to ensure her children got the opportunity to succeed. Thank you for instilling the values of education, hard work, dedication, and loyalty.

This book is also dedicated to my son, Jamison. From the day you were born, I knew my life would not be the same. I am proud to say that I am your father. I know you're going to do great things. I love you, Son.

CONTENTS

ACKNOWLEDGEMENTS

Thank you to Grandma Lillie Jones for always looking out and having loving and encouraging words. I know you are looking down from heaven and are proud of the legacy you left behind. I would like to thank the rest of my family because often you said things or did things that helped me become the person that I am today. Thank you to my brother and sister Erick and April Phillips for being the type of siblings anyone would love to have.

Thank you to my wife Kandice Phillips for all the love and support you have given me and for giving me our beautiful son Jamison, who provides balance and purpose in my life. I know he is going to do great things.

Thank you to Walter Turman for being a mentor, brother, and example of what it is to be a man and provider to one's family. Thank you to La'Darryl Hollingsworth for all your technical skills to help make this book and my other projects successful. Thank you to Alfonso Boyer for helping out when needed whether it was with videos, ideas, or just giving a laugh.

I would like to thank everyone who has ever made a positive contribution into my life. I would also like to thank those who made negative contributions, because you also motivated me to be who I am today.

INTRODUCTION

Adolescence can be a fun time! Your voice is getting deeper, you're growing taller, developing muscles, the young ladies are starting to look good to you, and the young ladies are starting to think *you look good*! In addition your parents are probably giving you a little more freedom; you're allowed to come home a little later, your parents probably leave you at home a few hours by yourself, you are entrusted with the responsibility of completing your homework on your own, and you may be allowed to start choosing and purchasing your own music and clothes. While these are just a few examples of the freedoms you may be given as you mature, the fact remains that you are just a few *short* years from "adulthood." This is important because during your transition into adulthood, you will be expected to take responsibility for your life, attend a college or a trade school, obtain employment, move out into a place of your own, and become a productive and contributing member of society. With these emerging freedoms come great responsibility and a period of time I like to call *Crunch Time.*

This period in your life is like the fourth quarter of a basketball game with five minutes left and the score is tied. Why? This is a time when your decisions become very important and can have a big impact on the outcome of the game, which is your life. Nothing is worse than a turnover or missed free throw at this critical point of the game. This is exactly why I wrote this book.

Sometimes during this period of life, some youth fall into what I classify as the *Traps*. Youths fall into traps by losing interest in school, participating in criminal activities, using drugs, joining gangs, losing confidence in their abilities, having sex, disrespecting their parents, or having other negative behaviors.

Adolescence is a time when you must try to be on point and remember to focus on the important things because one crucial mistake during this time can impact the outcome of the game—your life. This book will cover some of the most significant and avoidable traps that hinder youth from being successful and reaching their true potential. Before we go any deeper, let's discuss why we call these success-suppressing concepts "traps." *Webster* defines a trap as "a device or enclosure designed to catch and retain animals, typically by allowing entry but not exit or by catching hold of a part of." The important thing to remember about traps is that they are most dangerous if you are caught in one. Hence traps are avoidable if you steer clear of them. This is the purpose of this book, to identify the most common traps, help you steer clear of them, and help you escape the traps if you are temporarily captured. I say temporarily because it is never too late to make change, turn your life around, and grasp success. You must make a conscious decision to be successful. Read this book for understanding and complete the activities with your parents, friends, and other individuals who want you to experience success. **So let's get to it!**

Chapter 1
No Hunger Trap

"Doing the best at this moment puts you in the best place for the next moment." – Oprah Winfrey

Most people *say* they want to be successful. Hey, who doesn't want to make good grades, be on the school basketball team, and have big fancy houses, tight cars, fresh clothes, and sick retro shoes? Some may say they want all of these things, yet I often wonder, "How bad do you want them? How bad do you want success? How bad do you want good grades? How bad do you want to go to college? How bad do you want that scholarship? How hard are you willing to work? What are you willing to sacrifice? What friends are you willing to give up? Are you willing to hear and ignore the *hateration* from the haters? Are you willing to lose some sleep? What habits are you willing to break?"

The problem with attaining success is that while most people want to be successful, they aren't willing to do whatever it takes "legally" to succeed. Most people claim they want good grades, yet they aren't willing to stay up late and complete their homework. Often, eager athletes and novice players say they want to make it on the basketball or football team; however, most players aren't willing to go hard in the weight room or work on their game during the off seasons. A lot of people want to make good money, though they aren't willing to put in overtime on

1

their jobs, graduate from a training program/school, or seek legal alternatives to earning extra income. Many people want to be rappers, but they don't want to study the history of hip-hop in order to become better, nor do they want to put in time at the studio. Many people want to be successful until they realize they have to sacrifice some things. You may not be able to watch as much reality TV as you would like to. You may have to give up some video game time. You may have to lose some sleep or sacrifice some "homie time" and be more accountable and responsible. You can't just *want* to be successful; you have to *want it bad* and be willing to do **whatever it takes** to reach it.

Let me tell you how bad you have to want it. There's a story about a young man who wanted to be successful. He went to speak to a guru (someone who knows a lot), and he asked the guru what he could do to achieve success. The guru told the young man: "I don't normally do this, but meet me at the beach tomorrow morning at four a.m". The young man was puzzled as to why the guru wanted to meet at the beach to talk about success, but then he imagined the fancy cars and houses he'd have someday and agreed to meet the guru the next morning. The next day the young man arrived at the beach to see the guru awaiting him. At first the young man was confused and felt a little overdressed because he was wearing an expensive suit and the guru had on swim shorts and a beat-up T-shirt. He asked why they were at the beach, and the guru told the young man, "We are here to learn how to be successful." The guru asked the young man to follow him into the ocean.

The young man looked at the guru with a funny look on his face, but followed the guru into the ocean anyway. All he could think about was all the things he would be able to buy once he was successful. They walked into the ocean; first, their feet became wet, then they walked deeper and the water reached their knees. The guru walked deeper into the water, which was then waist-deep. Then they walked a little deeper and the water was neck high. All of a sudden, the guru grabbed the young man's head and forced him under water. The young man began screaming and trying to get the guru off of him. Time went by and the boy began to panic, thinking the guru was going to drown him, and then all of a sudden the guru let the young man go. The young man began screaming at the guru while trying to catch his breath. After catching his breath, the young man asked the guru what the heck he was doing. The guru responded, "What did you want to do when I had you under water?" The young man angrily said, "Breathe!" The guru responded, "That's it!" The young man grew angrier and started walking back toward the beach when he heard the guru say, "That's it. When you want to be successful as bad as you want to breathe, then you will be successful."

You see, wanting to be successful isn't something you can do part time or something you do when you *feel* like it. Success requires you to be very consistent and deliberate. It requires you to go to work when you don't want to, when you're sleepy, when the homies are kickin' it, when that TV show is on, or when your boys are playing video games with each other

3

online. I recently learned that if you want to be successful, you have to be willing to do what others are not. If you want to be the best baller, you have to be practicing when others are asleep. If you want to be the best video game designer, you need to go hard with creating unique concepts for games while others are merely playing games. You have to want success, live success, eat success, listen to success, watch success, surround yourself with success, and sleep success. Your life must revolve around doing things that will help you be successful: education, work, positive people, and other positive activities.

SO, HOW BAD DO YOU WANT IT? For our first activity, we're going to create a vision board and "Whys" for each item.

Let's create a vision board! Vision boards are very easy and simple to create. All you need is a poster board, glue, a few magazines you can cut images out of, a positive attitude, and an imagination. The idea is to surround yourself with images of who you want to become, things you want to achieve, what you want to have, where you want to live and so forth.

Steps To Create a Vision Board

1. Get several magazines that you can cut images out of.
2. Go through your magazines and tear out images, words, and phrases that get your attention. (No gluing yet, just make a pile of your images.)
3. Pick the images and phrases you like the most and lay them on the board in the order of your choice, leaving

4

the center of the board clear of magazine images.

4. Glue the images and phrases on the board and briefly write why this image or phrase is on the board. (Make sure it's a compelling reason!)

5. In the center space, paste an image of yourself.

6. Hang your vision board in an area you will see it often! (Bedroom, office, wall of your favorite room.)

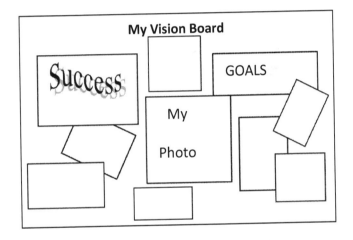

Chapter 2
No Goals Trap

"Education is the passport to the future, for tomorrow belongs to those who prepare for it today." – Malcolm X

There's a saying, "If you do not know where you're going, you'll probably end up somewhere else." To put it simply, it's important to know where you're going before you start walking or moving in any direction. Look, I don't know about you, but I am not going to get on a plane without first verifying it's headed where I want to go. I'm not trying to end up in Antarctica when I was trying to visit family in California. I'm not trying to be that guy dressed in short pants and sandals in Antarctica freezing my butt off. In life, setting **Good Goals** helps us get to our destinations. I know some of you may be thinking, *I don't know what I want to be*, or, *I'm too young to be setting goals*. What I'm here to tell you is, you're never too young to have dreams and set goals. It's okay to change your goals, but what is not okay is not having any goals at all.

Look, there are a number of people and things that can hold you back, like haters, the neighborhood where you live, and even people you thought had your back. Even so, the most important thing holding many of us back is not having good goals. Let's think about it for a minute. I'm sure a lot of you reading this book participate in sports or play an instrument, rap,

7

or dance, and I bet you have set goals and didn't even know it! How many of you tell yourselves, at the beginning of a basketball or football season, *I want to win at least ten games*, or, *I want to have a dunk this season.* Or, *I want to have at least ten sacks?* Guess what? You set a goal!

So what is a goal? A goal is simply something you want to achieve. Check this out. Before we start making goals, there are a few things to know such as making a distinction between goals and dreams. Often I hear people talk about the two as if they're interchangeable. Dreams are necessary to have, but the problem with dreams is that, by themselves, they're not very effective. Dreams are abstract concepts; in the English language, there are two main types of nouns, abstract and concrete nouns. Concrete nouns are nouns that can be seen or touched. Abstract nouns are nouns that cannot be seen or touched and are generally feelings or a state of being. Common examples of abstract nouns are anger, sadness, strength, and courage. Common examples of concrete nouns are things such as table, chair, and wall. You see, there's a huge difference between concrete and abstract nouns; one is in the physical and can be touched, while the other is more evasive and can't be touched. This is exactly why we have to transform these evasive and abstract dreams into tangible, physical goals by writing them down. Let's look at something many might think is a goal: *I want to get A's on my next report card.* That is a great thing to want to do, but there are some things that need to be set in place before you can achieve this goal. Let's look at a few things:

1. What are you going to do to get A's?
2. What things do you have to change to put you on a course to get A's?
3. Do you have to study longer?
4. Do you have to change your study habits?
5. Do you have to pay more attention in class?
6. Do you have to take more notes?

As you can see, before we create goals, we have to ask ourselves a few questions to get a better understanding of what we want to achieve and what we need to do to reach the goal. These types of questions help us make **Good Goals.** We don't just want to make lame goals; we want to make **Good Goals.** There are many ways to set goals, but here are some simple ways to do it:

1. Decide what you want to do. (Be ready to "make it do what it do." Don't be scurred!)
2. Decide what things you have to start doing **now** to achieve the goal. (Why wait? Start now! Just do it!)
3. Identify your resources. (People that can help you achieve your goal.) For example, a teacher, parent, or maybe a mentor.
4. Create small steps that help you get to your goal. (You can't eat a cow in one day; you have to eat a little bit each day.)
5. Decide how long you want it to take to finish your goal—a week, a month, or a year.
6. Create your goal. (Let's get it!)

Good Goals are very important. They keep you on track and help you get places you never thought you could. Remember, if you're having trouble setting good goals, there are a number of people you can go to for help (teachers, school social workers, school counselors, your principals, pastor, and other people that you look up to). So, let's set some good goals. Let's get it! (Refer to the Good Goals activity.)

Good Goals Activities (GGA)

As mentioned previously, it's important to set **Good Goals**, not just any goals. Good Goals help us reach our destinations in life because they help us identify what we want to achieve and the steps we're going to take to achieve these goals. After you write down your goals, hang them in your locker and bedroom. Let's set some goals!

What do you want to achieve?

_____

_____

What will the final outcome look like?

_____

_____

How long will it take to achieve these goals? (E.g., Two weeks)

_____

_____

What small steps are you going to start doing right now to achieve these goals? (E.g., Study two hours a day.)

_____

_____

_____

_____

Reaffirm your goals! (I will…)

_____

_____

_____

_____

In school, you're provided with an academic report every four and a half weeks. The first being a progress report, the second being a report card. You're given a total of four progress reports and four report cards throughout the course of a full academic school year. Use each academic report as a timeline to revisit your goals and identify how close to or how far you are from achieving them. Use the second part of this exercise to determine if you are or are not accomplishing your goals, or at least moving closer toward them.

(1st report period)

Did I reach my goal?   Yes or No
Am I close to reaching my goal?   Yes or No
Why, didn't I reach my goal?

_____

_____

_____

What do I need to do differently to get closer to reaching my goal?

_____

_____

(2nd report period)

Did I reach my goal?   Yes or No
Am I close to reaching my goal?   Yes or No
Why, didn't I reach my goal?

_____

_____

_____

What do I need to do differently to get closer to reaching my goal?

_____

_____

_____

(3rd report period)

Did I reach my goal?   Yes or No
Am I close to reaching my goal?   Yes or No
Why, didn't I reach my goal?

_____

_____

_____

What do I need to do differently to get closer to reaching my goal?

_____

_____

_____

(4th report period)

Did I reach my goal?   Yes or No
Am I close to reaching my goal?   Yes or No
Why, didn't I reach my goal?

_____

_____

_____

What do I need to do differently to get closer to reaching my goal?

_____

_____

_____

_____

Chapter 3
The YOLO Trap

"Action expresses priorities." – Mahatma Gandhi

Everyone on this planet, whether rich or poor, is afforded the same twenty-four hours a day. Even though 50 Cent has major money, fancy cars, and nice houses, he still gets the same twenty-four hours you do. Even Microsoft founder Bill Gates, whose net worth is estimated to be sixty-nine billion dollars, still has the same twenty-four hours you do. Even Jay Z, a successful hip-hop artist and business man, whose estimated worth is 400 million dollars, still only gets the same twenty-four hours we do. To take it a step further, the homeless person you may have seen last week on the corner or under a bridge has the same twenty-four-hour days that you do. So what's the difference between the successful people and people who are not successful? The difference is that they don't let any and everything into their lives. To keep it simple, the reason they're successful is that they maximize their twenty-four hours. They squeeze all the toothpaste out the tube, so to speak. They squeeze all the juice out of the lemon. You know how it is when you have a bag of chips and you only have a few crumbs left, what do you do? You straighten the bag up, tilt your head back, and tap the bag on your lips to get all the crumbs out. Well, that's what you have to do with your twenty-four hours.

You have to maximize all of your time and get all those chips out the bag. So now that you've had your bag of chips, I have a question for you. How are you going to spend the majority of your time? Will it be playing video games, surfing the Internet, listening to music, texting, and tweeting, or will it be studying, working on your game, reading, hitting the weight room, and spending time with successful people?

Let me break it down for you. A few years ago, when rap artist 50 Cent first came out, he hit the music industry by storm. He had crazy diss records, looked like he could knock anybody out, and talked mad reckless. The craziest thing about his success was that he had things poppin' off in all types of areas, a successful debut album that went diamond (sold ten million records), a clothing line, a shoe line, video game, movie, soundtrack to the movie, and a record label. Man, when he first came out, everyone was walking around saying, "G-G-G-G Unit..." Yeah, even me! He was making so much money from so many different areas because of one reason: he maximized his twenty-four hours! 50 didn't waste time. During an interview he was asked when he found time to sleep, because he had so much going on, and 50 responded, "I don't get sleep because sleep is for people who don't want to make money!" 50 learned what many other successful people know: if you want to be successful in the classroom, on the court, on the field, in college, and in life, you can't just let anything or anyone have your time. You have to be selective with it because it's one of the most valuable things you have. Someone once told me that the only thing that is certain is death. The time on this earth is finite; therefore, it's one of the most valuable things that you have. Growing up, my friends and I used to share clothes and shoes to make it look like we had more clothes than we did, but do you think I shared my freshest clothes and shoes? Of course I didn't. You wouldn't loan out your best pieces, even to your boys. So, why would you let everyone and everything have all your time? When your homies want to kick it, make sure you've finished your work first. When they're playing video games at all hours of the night, work on something that's going to better you and take you to the next level. The makers of *Call of Duty* made their money by maximizing their time. The creators of *Madden* have made their money by maximizing their time. What are you going to do to get yours? What are you going to do to make yourself successful? Are you willing to maximize your time, because the truth is, You Only Live Once (YOLO).

Let's look at how you spend your twenty-four hours! Let's see if the way you spend your twenty-four hours is consistent with achieving your goals and being successful!

Take out a sheet of paper, using the chart on the next page, record your daily activities.

Time	How Do You Spend Your Time?
5:00 a.m.	
6:00 a.m.	
7:00 a.m.	
8:00 a.m.	
9:00 a.m.	
10:00 a.m.	
11:00 a.m.	
12:00 p.m.	
1:00 p.m.	
2:00 p.m.	
3:00 p.m.	
4:00 p.m.	
5:00 p.m.	
6:00 p.m.	
7:00 p.m.	
8:00 p.m.	
9:00 p.m.	
10:00 p.m.	
11:00 p.m.	
12:00 a.m.	

What patterns of how you spend your time do you notice?

_____

_____

_____

_____

List the things you spend one hour or more doing.

_____

_____

_____

_____

The things you spend one hour or more doing, are they helping you reach the goals you mentioned earlier in the book? If not, write down what you could be doing instead to maximize your time. (Hint: We can all maximize our time better.)

_____

_____

_____

_____

Write down three solid responses you can use when people approach you to do something that's not consistent with what you are trying to accomplish. For example, "I can't meet you guys over there; I have to babysit my little brother."

_____

_____

_____

_____

Chapter 4
The No "Heart" Trap

"Without a struggle, there can be no progress."
– Frederick Douglas

Man, I am tired of this! This teacher hates me! I hate this school! This class is too difficult! I was never good at math! I'm just going to drop this class before the drop deadline! Why even try? I am not going to be able to do this. Nobody else in my family graduated from college! I can't start my own business! I don't have the money to start this business! I can't lose this weight! These are common words I hear among students, youth, and even adults when things get tough and they're faced with challenges. Often people use challenges as excuses to give up or justify not putting forth any real effort because, in their eyes, it's easier to just call it quits than to persevere and make something happen. So why do people make excuses? Some of the reasons might include laziness, trying too hard to "save face," having too much "SWAG" to struggle, fear, worrying about what others might think, and embarrassment. Before we go any further, I want you to think about something. When was the last time you heard or saw someone repeatedly tell themselves they couldn't do something or quit when they were faced with a challenge? Think about that person for a moment.

Continue thinking of this self-doubting person and the energy they spend with the negative self-talk they speak openly. Is this person successful? Have they achieved or conquered anything of significance such as good grades, having a starting position on a sports team, winning awards, or received accolades for any accomplishments? If the answer is no, chances are that the person is unsuccessful because they've developed a cancerous pattern of quitting that keeps them from being successful. The reason I call this process cancerous is because if you start quitting and making excuses in one area of your life, it will start to creep into other areas.

For example, consider someone that is gaining weight. Initially, the gain might just be noticeable a little in the stomach area, but then as they continue to put on more weight, the pounds start to show up in their arms, under the neck, on their legs, and nearly every other part of the body. The same is true for not having heart, or not being dedicated to your success, and giving up. First, you quit the football team because you are not getting enough playing time, then you stop going to math class because it may be difficult, then you start skipping one day a week from school and then you stop going to school all together. You see, becoming a quitter and not having heart is a gradual process that starts with quitting small things and ends with making the choice to quit bigger challenges. I am not going to front and pretend like I haven't quit or made excuses before, but I stopped making excuses when I realized that excuses only hinder you from reaching your full potential and that the only way to be successful is to work hard and persevere through obstacles. While it may be scary to try something new and take on a new challenge, or even a little embarrassing not to accomplish something you set out to do, it's okay. The fact that you attempted to tackle the challenge is laying the foundation that will help you become a success story. Sometimes, when I'm faced with challenges, I read about success stories. Believe it or not, they help motivate me to keep going. Entrepreneurs, doctors, lawyers, individuals involved in the music industry, professional athletes, and media personalities all have one thing in common: they persevered when faced with obstacles. They Do Not Give Up Nor Do They Allow Others To Convince Them To Give Up! They have heart!

Let's look at a few success stories. Michael Jordan, the greatest basketball player of all time, was cut from his high school basketball team before eventually making the team the following year. He went on to attend North Carolina University and play in the NBA. Not only was Michael Jordan a great basketball player, but off the court, Michael had a great impact on the game of basketball. He changed the popularity of the game, both nationally and internationally. Before Michael Jordan, people in other countries really weren't as interested in basketball. By the time Michael was finished, he had everyone wanting to dunk and stick their tongues out while they were playing the sport. As a result of Michael increasing the popularity of basketball internationally, the NBA now has many international players, including Dirk Nowitzki, Steve Nash, Manu Ginobili, Tony Parker, and Ricky Rubio.

Michael Jordan's success on the court also made him one of the most marketable brands, which led to endorsements from Nike, Gatorade, and Hanes underwear. In addition to these endorsements, Michael also owns several car dealerships, an NBA franchise team (Charlotte Bobcats), and his own shoe line, Jumpman. A few of the professional athletes signed with Jordan's shoe company include: Chris Paul, Carmelo Anthony, Blake Griffin, Derek Jeter, Jimmy Rollins, and many more. Hey, chances are you have or have had a pair of Michael's retro shoes. But here is the kicker: Michael's current net worth is estimated at 1 billion dollars. That's a lot of cheese! Ask yourself where Michael would be if he'd given up when his high school basketball coach cut him from the team. How would the game of basketball have been impacted if Michael called it quits? How hard do you think Michael worked when his coach cut him from the team? Aye... you are capable of making things happen also! Let's check out the next success story.

Robert Johnson was the first African American billionaire. I know what you're thinking, *Who the heck is Robert Johnson?* Well, he's the individual that founded Black Entertainment Television, or BET, as you probably know it. It's the cable station with *106 & Park* and *The Game* on its roster of current shows. Robert started BET with hard work and $15,000 of his own money, plus the help of a few investors.

Eventually Robert sold BET to a huge media company, Viacom, for **three billion dollars**. Yes, three *billion*, not million. He later went on to be one of the few minorities to have majority ownership of a professional basketball team, the Charlotte Bobcats, which he later sold to the great Michael Jordan. Like Michael Jordan, Robert Johnson has heart!

To really help you understand how successful Robert was, I want to emphasize what it means to be a majority owner. A majority owner is someone who has the most ownership of a business or company, while a minority owner is someone who owns a tiny portion of a business. Think of it like this, let's say I have a large pizza with eight slices and I give you one slice while I keep the other seven slices. You may have a portion of the pizza, but you have a much smaller share. This is the basic premise of being a minority owner versus a majority owner. Because I had seven slices, I'd be the majority owner and since you'd only have one slice, you would be a minority stakeholder. There are many examples of individuals who own minority stakes in businesses and companies. For example, Jay Z has a minority stake with the Brooklyn Nets. Nelly has a minority stake with the Charlotte Bobcats, and the list goes on and on. I say this to help you understand how much money and net worth it requires to be able to be a majority owner of a sports team and to show how hard someone has to work to get this type of success. The fact that Robert Johnson was a majority owner is a huge accomplishment. Quitting would not have allowed for such success.

These stories and countless others of those who chose to fight through their challenges inspired me when I was faced with one of my greatest challenges. While in graduate school getting my master's degree, I lost my job. As a result I was in a huge financial bind. Important questions had to be answered. How would I pay rent? How would I eat? How would I put gas in my car to make it to school, and how would I get another job that would fit my school schedule of classes and an internship during the day? The biggest questions I had to ask myself were if I'd stay in school or if I'd quit and get a job. I decided that I'd stay in school, but I can remember the challenges and barriers I faced like it was yesterday. I remember putting three dollars of gas in my 1993 Yamaha FZR motorcycle, hoping I could make it from home to school and from school back home. I can remember running out of gas several times on the freeway and having to call for roadside service. I remember eating peanut butter and jelly sandwiches and Top Ramen noodles for breakfast, lunch, and dinner. I remember wearing the same shoes and clothes because I didn't have money to buy new stuff often. Even so, what I remember most was graduation and when my diploma was available for pick up. It said *Patrick Phillips, Graduate of Georgia State University, School of Social Work*. Those few words made my struggles so worth it. Let's keep it real, the easiest thing would have been to quit school and get a full-time job, but instead I had heart and fought for my education. I pushed and chose to go to school on days I did not feel like going. It was a choice to eat foods that fit my budget at the time. I made a conscious choice to have heart and stay positive, even when the bills came in the mail, many times attached to late notices. I chose to go to school when I had many things on my mind. Martin Luther King Jr. stated, "The ultimate measure of a man is not where he stands in moments of comfort and convenience, but where he stands at times of challenge and controversy." My question to you is where do you stand when things are hard? How bad do you want to succeed? How much heart do you have? How bad do you want to change your situation? How far are you willing to go to make sure you're successful? Where do you stand in times of controversy and difficulty? Do you stand with defeat and quitting or do you stand with strength and perseverance? Hey, you are reading my book so I know you're headed in a positive direction.

To end this chapter, I want to provide several motivational and inspirational quotes that will help you stay motivated and encouraged when things get tough. I want you to choose three and put one in your locker, one in your school folder or frequently visited safe place, and one in your bedroom (wall, mirror, desk, etc.).

QUOTES

"Death is not the greatest loss in life. The greatest loss is what dies inside while still alive. Never surrender."
– 2 Pac

"I am not afraid of dying. I am afraid of not trying."
– Jay Z

"It's hard to beat a person who never gives up."
– Babe Ruth

"Don't count the days, make the days count."
– Muhammad Ali

"Many of life's failures are people who did not realize how close they were to success when they gave up."
– Thomas A. Edison

"When you come to the end of your rope, tie a knot and hang on."
– Franklin D. Roosevelt

"I'd rather die enormous than live dormant."
– Jay Z

"Remind yourself. Nobody built like you; you designed yourself."
– Jay Z

"It does not matter how slowly you go as long as you do not stop."
– Confucius

"I'm obsessed with perfection. I want to work. I don't want to take this for granted."
– Drake

"There are no shortcuts to any place worth going."
– Beverly Sills

"Success seems to be largely a matter of hanging on after others have let go."
– William Feather

"I am a slow walker, but I never walk back."
– Abraham Lincoln

"Most people never run far enough on their first wind to find out they've got a second."
– William James

Chapter 5
The No "Why" Trap

"There are no shortcuts to any place worth going."
– Beverly Sills

Parents will tell you that one of the biggest challenges and most interesting times in parenthood is when little children discover the word "why." The reason for this is because children never stop asking why questions—*Why is the sky blue? Why is the earth round? Why are people different colors? Why are people short? Why is he so ugly?* Unfortunately, as we get older, we lose our curiosity in discovering why. Interestingly, this is the reason so many people are unable to find their niche, their happiness, success and why they're often uncomfortable with themselves. Before you can realistically go out and go hard for what you want to accomplish, you must first establish a reason so strong and compelling that when things are going badly, you still want to "go hard." Let me break it down.

I'm sure many of us have seen the movie *300* or heard of the story where 300 Spartans fend off a massive Persian army for several days, buying Greece time to build its military. Yes, I'm talking about the movie where Leonidas kicks the Persians down the bottomless pit and yells, "This is Sparta!" In the movie Leonidas takes 300 Spartans and several hundred more Greeks to the "Hot Gates," a location in the mountains so narrow that when

31

the massive Persian army arrives, they're not able to use their superior numbers to defeat Leonidas and his men. You see, the reason this story is so interesting and has been passed down for hundreds of years is because Leonidas and his supporters made a conscious decision to face hundreds and even thousands of Persian soldiers, even though they knew they were outnumbered and might be killed. Many people would've looked at Leonidas like he was crazy if he asked them to join his small army to take on an army that was much larger. They would have said. *"Naw, I ain't going with you over there."* Fear regarding what if and why would have overcome them.

Underneath all the interesting facts around Leonidas and the Battle of Thermopylae lies a three-letter word that explains the purpose of this battle's occurrence, and it's what the Spartans and several other Greek city-states had, which was "why." They were willing to make personal sacrifices, including facing death, leaving their wives, children, parents, brothers, and sisters behind, because they had a rationale or reason that made all of their sacrifices worth it. The answer to all of their why questions was worth it. *Why go through a battle knowing you might not win?* For them, their responses included protecting their homeland and their way of life, their wives, their children, and their culture. Though this event occurred many years ago, the concept of having a compelling "why" is still relevant to life today. In order to do something with heart, you have to be able to honestly answer the why questions with a response that's worth it for you. I challenge you to ask and answer the "why" questions surrounding decisions you make on a daily basis. Having a "why" question, and an answer that makes sense to you, increases your fortitude for being successful. It'll keep you going when you're sleepy and don't want to do homework, it'll keep you going hard when the homies are kicking it versus focusing or making good decisions, and it'll make you hold it down when you don't feel like studying. Look, I can't give you a "why", because it's something you have to find yourself; however, I will share some "whys" of my life.

Growing up in a single-parent household in the hood of Los Angeles (LA) was really hard. We lived a little bit of everywhere: Inglewood, Long Beach, and South Central, which were all the parts of California you don't see during those nice awards shows like the Grammys or on vacation postcards. There was gang violence, homelessness, poverty, poor schools, and limited opportunities. I remember my mom moved a lot when we were younger, to move us to the best of the worst schools in our school district. Yes, I meant what I said; she tried to get us in the best schools possible, but many of them were not good environments. I remember how much she sacrificed. She quit her job at the post office and worked jobs that required less hours, which meant lower pay so she could be home with us when we got out of school. She didn't buy herself a lot of nice things because she wanted her children to look nice. She also spent hours with us on homework and at basketball and track practices to provide us with positive outlets. I could spend hours telling you stories about the sacrifices she made, but I am sure you get the point. I couldn't let my mother's sacrifices go in vain, so I tried my best to avoid doing anything that would ruin all of her hard work. I went to class on time and generally tried to make good grades. Yes, there were a few times she had to get on me, but I did my best not to mess things up.

Today, my "whys" for going hard are still the same, but I've added a few more causes for my reasons; they are my wife and newborn son. I have to make positive things happen to ensure my family has what they need. I challenge you to find something so strong and important to you that, no matter what is going on, you have the resolve to persevere. I challenge you to keep going when things seem hard. Your "why" might be your younger brother or sister who is watching your every move. It might be all the sacrifices your parents have made for you. It might be your friend who lost his life. Or it might even be the fact that you're fed up with your present situation. I challenge you to look yourself in the mirror daily and say, boldly and confidently, "I AM GOING TO MAKE THIS HAPPEN." I challenge you to keep going when everyone is "hatin'." I challenge you to keep going when you feel like giving up. I challenge you to keep going when you're tired. I never ask anything of anyone that I know they can't do. I have **major faith** in you! Let's make it happen, because failure is not an option!

Chapter 6
The Poor Decisions Trap

"It's amazing how much trouble you can get in when you don't have anything else to do." – Quincy Jones

What do you do with your spare time? Do you play video games? Do you hoop? Do you rap? Do you read? Do you play board games? Do you surf the Internet? Do you play an instrument? I know it feels good to chill and hang out, but did you know that even the smallest choices you make have consequences? Have you ever eaten too much candy and gotten sick? Have you ever eaten so much food at Christmas or Thanksgiving dinner that you got ill and your stomach hurt? We can laugh about it and I'll admit, these may be silly examples, but I'm sure we have all done at least one of these things. I give these examples to help you see that even the smallest choices that we make have consequences. Before we start talking about consequences, let's not forget that there are both positive and negative consequences. Positive consequences are things like working on your game every day after practice, then hitting the game-winning shot right before the buzzer rings in the championship game. Negative consequences are things like not working on your game and losing the championship game because you missed the free throw that could have tied the game in overtime.

Every day you're given opportunities to make decisions—things like what to eat for breakfast, Takis or Hot Fries, Coke or Sprite, to do or not do your homework, who to hang out with, to go or not to go to class, and many other choices. The point here is that **you are in control of many of the things that occur to you daily.** Everyday young adults make poor decisions, like not doing homework, not going to class, deciding to do drugs, fighting, joining gangs, disrespecting their parents, and a number of other things. You see these children daily because you witness them fighting, leaving campus during school hours, doing crimes, and coming home at all hours of the night. To show you how real making poor decisions can be, let me share this with you.

While in high school, I played on the basketball team with an individual we're going to call Paul. Paul had long, curly hair, was quick as lightning, had a sick jump shot, and used to cross people over so bad. When he played, he made everybody guarding him look like they were sorry. It was almost like he was in *The Matrix* and could do things on the court that others could not! Paul was on a totally different level. I'm gonna keep it real, Paul was very popular and had all the ladies; he was "that dude." Even though he was doing it big and had so much potential, Paul smoked marijuana and maintained that he was in a gang. Even with all of this, Paul received a scholarship to a Division I university. While at the university, Paul didn't spend much time focusing on school because he thought he was good enough to play in the NBA. He continued to do drugs and not complete his school assignments. Even though Paul was hoop'n, the school wanted someone that could really hold it down, both academically and athletically. The university then signed the top guard in the state where the college was located. Paul left the college because he was afraid to lose his starting position. He tried to transfer to another college, but his grades were so low that he couldn't be accepted into the school. Paul trained very hard and tried to play professionally overseas, but no one would sign him. Paul is now nearly thirty years old and plays on a bootleg semiprofessional basketball team. Paul has no degree to show for his years in college, no steady income, and a very low quality of life. Paul continues to smoke marijuana and chase a dream of being a professional athlete that is long gone because of his poor decisions like using drugs, not taking school seriously, and not having a backup plan.

Listen, the decisions you make now will affect you later in life. Do you think people that are homeless, addicted to drugs and in jail want to be in their situations? Do you think people who beg for money on the street like it? Do you think people who are addicted to drugs and sleeping in abandoned houses like it? Do you think that when they were youth, they said, "I want to grow up and be a junkie?" Many of them made decisions that affected them as children, young adults, and later as adults, decisions that may have led to their present situations. Many of you might be asking, "What can I do now to make positive decisions for my life now and later?" Positive decisions can include taking school seriously, staying away from drugs, involving yourself in positive activities such as athletics, the arts, school clubs, finding positive adults that you can speak with when things aren't going well, setting good goals, and keeping positive friends (<u>not those in gangs, doing drugs, or who don't value their education</u>). Keeping positive friends is important because if they don't do positive things, they won't encourage you to do positive things. There are many other things that you can do to remain positive. Speak with your parents, teachers, school counselor, principal, and other adults that you feel comfortable with to find out more options. **<u>The positive people around you want you to be successful, and they have no problem helping you. All you have to do is ask.</u>**

Chapter 7
The Homie Trap

"The wisest men follow their own direction."
– Euripides

Children learn a lot from their peers. Not only do children learn a lot from their friends, but they're also easily influenced by their peers. It's this influence that can create a situation where people believe or do something just because everyone else is doing it. **Often pressures to "fit in" cause children to do things that they normally wouldn't do.** You bully someone because everyone else is doing it. You try drugs because your boys are using them. You skip class because the dudes with "swag" are doing it. You're stealing because you're trying to keep up with what everyone else has. You join a gang because it looks cool.

One of the most interesting things about peer pressure is that it's not always obvious; it can be subliminal, meaning that pressure to do things may not be easy to recognize when it begins. Often in commercials they show someone walking over to another person and saying something like, "Smoke this joint, man," but peer pressure doesn't always happen this way. **Sometimes people say things directly to you, while other times peer pressure occurs simply because your friends do things and you participate just because you're around them.**

I remember one such occurrence very vividly. Several years ago, five of my friends and I were supposed to go out and hit a club. Before we went out, one of my friends wanted to stop by this one location to "make some quick money." Another friend and I did not want to go because this particular part of town was not a safe place to be late at night. Unfortunately the rest of the group was able to pressure and convince us to go anyway. I remember them telling us it would be a "quick run." After arriving at this large apartment complex, my friend began to gamble with several other people there. I can remember thinking how it was not unusual for fights and altercations to break out during situations like this. Not more than five minutes later, the police burst into the apartment complex. My friends and I were snatched up by the police because everyone else in the complex was able to run into their apartments.

All I could remember thinking was how I had told my friends just minutes before that this was not the place to be. The weirdest and scariest part of the evening was when the police handcuffed us and took us to the alley behind the apartment complex. At the time all I could think about was the police either beating us in the alley where no one could see or them planting something on us so they could take us to jail. I can remember how the police made us lay face down on the ground in the dirty alley where people threw trash, used the bathroom, and did all other types of things. While on the ground, the police searched us all and eventually let us go. I remember getting up from the ground and my clothes were filthy. One of my friends was forced to lie in a nasty puddle of water and got up all muddy. Even though we all felt violated and punked, I remember thinking that things could have been much worse in that dark alley. The police could have done all kinds of things to us and nobody would have known. The only thing we really suffered that night was embarrassment and dirty clothes.

Unfortunately, there are many children throughout America who are not as lucky when they make mistakes and allow peer pressure to influence their decisions. There are many children and youth whose bad choices lead to serious consequences, such as going to jail, drug and alcohol addiction, being injured, and even death. How many times have we seen youth walking around with "R.I.P." or "Free the Homies" T-shirts? Listen, a "R.I.P." or "Free the Homies" shirt is not a badge of honor, nor does it mean anything to your parents and family. They would much rather have you there by their side, rather than dead or in jail. While death and incarceration may seem like extreme examples, the fact remains that everyday people make decisions they normally wouldn't due to peer pressure.

Let me share an experience with you. Many people know I like to ride motorcycles, and I actually used to be in a bike club. It is customary that if another bike crew had a member get injured or die while riding, other bike crews show support by meeting at the clubhouse where the injured rider was a member.

One summer another bike crew had a member who was killed while riding very fast trying to keep up with his crew. As customary, my bike crew went to their clubhouse and people were walking around drinking, partying, and having a good time just like nothing had happened. The saddest part about the whole situation was that the person that died had a one-year-old child. I remember thinking that this so-called "get together" to "show love" wouldn't provide any comfort to the family of the young man who died while riding, nor would it provide that young child with a father. The meeting would mean nothing a week later while everyone was at the next party "gettin' it in."

I eventually stopped riding with the crew because I soon had a child and I wanted to ride with people who were a little more responsible. The point here is that the decisions you make can hurt you and your family! No one will feel the stress like your mother, your brother, your sister, your father, or your grandmother. Your family members will be the ones crying and feeling the pain if something happens to you.

I want you to ask yourself about the last time you made a decision because you were pressured into it. What was the outcome? Was it worth it? Did you feel silly afterward? More often than not, after time passes, many people wish they hadn't made that decision. The lesson is to watch who you hang out with and don't be pressured into doing things that have negative consequences. There is nothing wrong with taking a stand and putting yourself first, because **"if you don't stand for something, you will fall for anything."**

Parents, it's impossible to prevent your children from ever being influenced by peer pressure, but there are a number of things that you can do to help. Parents, you can encourage a sense of pride and self-respect by providing creative outlets to your children such as sports, clubs, and a variety of other positive activities. This is recommended because children are less likely to participate in negative activities when they have positive outlets. Parents, you can also talk to your children about the risks of peer pressure. These conversations help because children have several life experiences, yet they're often unaware of the long-term impact of their decisions during those experiences. You can help them understand the dangers and traps of peer pressure. Get to know your child/children's friends. There is a saying that your friends are a reflection of you. This remains the same for children and teens.

My last and favorite recommendation is "keep it real." We all have experienced peer pressure as children, teens, and young adults. When you keep it real and tell your children about some of your personal experiences with peer pressure, you have an opportunity not only to strengthen your bond with your child, but also to create a channel for open communication, which is very beneficial. It was the rapport and basic foundation provided by my mother that allowed me to realize the wrongs of my actions when I started participating in potentially fatal behaviors. To the parents with children that have allowed peer pressure to cause them to make poor decisions **DO NOT GIVE UP ON THEM**.

Your child needs you more now than ever before. You can show how much you care and love your children by being supportive in their moments of greatest need. Let them know that their current mistakes do not mean they're unable to recover. I have always been a firm believer that if you fall, do a few push-ups and get up stronger. Learn from your mistakes and become a better person because of them. Let's take a look at who you hang with.

Are You Guilty By Association? (GBA) Activity

They say we're all a reflection of the people we spend the most time with. Put simply, the people that you hang out with generally share many of the same characteristics, hobbies, and philosophies that you have; otherwise, you probably wouldn't be friends nor spend much time together. While there's nothing wrong with having things in common with friends and people you share time with, the problems arise when the people you hang out with have negative characteristics and negative hobbies. Unfortunately, some people rarely look at the individuals they hang out with as possible causes for them not achieving their full potential. You will complete this assessment with your parent(s) or guardian. We will abbreviate the term "Guilty by Association" to "GBA." You are going to analyze your friends and see if you should really have these people as friends. Let's get to it!

List five of your closest friends and identify their

personal characteristics. (Remember characteristics are things like whether someone is lazy, negative, positive, honest, ambitious, dependable, dishonest, a hard worker, etc.)

"Friend" #1
Characteristics
-
-
-

"Friend" #2
Characteristics
-
-
-

"Friend" #3
Characteristics
-
-
-

"Friend" #4
Characteristics
-
-
-

"Friend" #5
Characteristics
-
-
-

Assessment:
Are the characteristics that you identified negative or positive? Explain:

_____
_____
_____

Are these "friends" people you want to be associated with?
Explain:

_____

_____

_____

Do these friends try to get you to do negative or positive things?
Explain:

_____

_____

_____

So now we're down to the million-dollar questions: What are you going to do? Do the characteristics of your "friends" listed above help you reach your goals, or do they hinder you from reaching your goals? After viewing your friends' characteristics, are you still happy to call these people your "friends?" If not, then you and your parents have some decisions to make. You have decisions to make because these are people you may decide to no longer associate with. Your parents have decisions to make because they can now be proactive in figuring out how to get you active in positive organizations/groups and supporting you by getting to know your circle of friends.

Chapter 8
Get Your Mind Right

"Whether you think you can, or you think you can't—you're right."
—Henry Ford

Life presents challenges in many forms: our environments, daily circumstances, challenging classes, well-known haters, and many other situations. With all of these challenges, the most important factor that determines how well we overcome these challenges is not money, resources, intelligence, wealth, or connections. While these factors will definitely help you get through some obstacles, the most important aspect is your mindset. Our mindset determines how well we deal with challenges and whether or not we are able to bounce back. Think of it like this, we've all seen basketball games where the game is tied and someone is at the free throw line shooting two free throws and the person misses the first one. In situations like this, there are two types of people; the first type thinks that because they missed the first free throw, they will miss the second. The second type says, "I know I missed the first one, so I am definitely not going to miss the second one." As we can see, there are two different approaches to the same situation; the first person approaches the situation with a defeated attitude while the second person challenges themselves to rise up to the occasion.

One pictures himself missing the second free throw while the other pictures himself making the second free throw. So my question to you is this: Which approach do you use when faced with a challenge? Do you picture yourself graduating high school or not graduating high school? Do you picture yourself making the team or not making the team? Do you picture yourself passing the class or not passing the class? Do you picture yourself being successful or not successful? In situations where people say you won't graduate, you'll be just like your father, you won't amount to anything, when the streets are calling, when your parents are getting on your nerves, when you just feel like giving up, I want you to say to yourself, "Get Your Mind Right." It's not what people say about you, it's whether you accept their view of who you are, what you can do, or who you become that makes the difference in your mindset.

So, how do we get our minds right when things seem like they are just going badly, when you feel like you can't pass that class, when you feel like doing something crazy because you're upset, when things just seem like they will never get better? You do it by visualizing how things are going to look when things get better, by viewing your present situation as a challenge and not as an obstacle, and by using affirmations. I know that you may be asking, "What do you mean 'visualizing how things are going to look,' and what are affirmations?" It's much easier than you think. There is a scene in the movie *X-Men: First Class* where Magneto (the mutant that can move metal with his mind) is learning how to use his powers by moving a large satellite. In the scene, Magneto doubts he can move the large satellite because he had never moved anything that big before. Magneto is told to visualize himself moving the satellite. His mindset is on visualizing himself moving the satellite though he's not sure how he'll do it. Eventually, Magneto begins to move the satellite. You see, the first thing Magneto had to do before he could actually move the satellite was to visualize himself doing it. The same thing pertains to you! You have to visualize yourself overcoming your challenges and turn negative statements into positive ones.

Instead of saying, "No one in my whole family has graduated from high school," **I want you to visualize yourself walking across the graduation stage.** Instead of saying, "College is for smart people, and I'm not smart," **I want you to visualize yourself holding your college diploma.** Instead of saying, "I hate math," **I want you to visualize the money you will be counting when you finish school.** Instead of saying, "This class is hard and I know I won't pass," **I want you to visualize yourself passing the final exam.**

The last part of getting our minds right is speaking positivity into our lives through affirmations. Even though life may be difficult at times and people may say hurtful things to us, one of the biggest obstacles keeping us from reaching success is negative self-talk. How often have we told ourselves things like, *you are not smart, you can't pass that class, you are fat, you are not as smart as them, you don't have what it takes?* This negative self-talk often prevents us from reaching our goals because we get scared. As a result of fear, we talk ourselves out of trying new things and get stuck doing things we are comfortable with. We can never grow and accomplish all that we are capable of if we are too afraid to get out of our comfort zone. So let's get our minds right.

Positive Affirmations

I have every bit as much brightness to offer the world as the next person.

I matter and what I have to offer this world also matters.

I have the smarts and the ability to get through this.

I am filled with energy, vitality, and high self-esteem.

I forgive myself for any and all past mistakes.

1. Write down two negative statements you've recently made about yourself. Then write a positive statement for each of the negative statements.

N:_____

P:_____

N:_____

P:_____

2. Create three affirmations you're going to say daily.

3. Choose at least one positive statement and one affirmation. Write them on separate sheets of paper and place them in conspicuous locations (e.g., notebook, locker, gym bag, bedroom, in your phone, etc.). Read the affirmation and positive statement daily.

4. Every two weeks switch positive statements and affirmations.

Chapter 9
Delinquent Criminal Activity Trap

"An error doesn't become a mistake until you refuse to correct it." – Orlando A.

Did you know that jails and prisons have become big business? People are "profiting" because they buy stocks in companies that build and manage prisons. These companies have made so much money because they've been able to target where to build new prisons. It may seem crazy, but some argue that these companies make predictions by looking at low test scores of elementary students and predicating that these children will have a good chance of going to jail someday.

The thought process behind this is that if you cannot read, do math, or perform arithmetic, you have very few options besides stealing, robbing, and killing—all paths that lead you to prison. There may be people out there *hoping* you don't go to class, hoping you don't do your homework, and hoping you give up and drop out so they can put you in a cell somewhere. Unfortunately, many students in middle school begin making decisions that will lead them down a road of criminal activity. Let's keep it real, no one is born a "thug"; no one is born a "G." It starts with children being around people doing bad things where they live. Young men become interested in these bad things that seem cool. It leads to them saying, "I want to be

59

like that," because the gangstas have "street cred," "swag," and all the ladies. This then leads to youth hanging out with negative people and doing negative things. Often times, parents notice changes in their child's behavior, such as staying out late, absences adding up at school, a drop in grades, and some even suspect drug usage. (**Parents: when you first begin to see these signs, it's time to intervene.**)

Here's an example. Several years ago I found out that someone I used to go to school with was sentenced to fifteen years in jail! This person, who I will call John, was caught transporting drugs. It turns out that John had been transporting drugs for several years and finally got caught when he was driving from one state to another and was pulled over for speeding. After being pulled over, the police found many pounds of marijuana and cocaine in his car. When I found out that John was in jail, I was shocked because during the time that I knew him in school, he was a cool person. I found out that after we graduated, John started hanging out with "shady" people. These people talked him into transporting drugs to make some "quick money." As you can see, these people who John once called "friends" got him "caught up" big time. By the time John gets out of jail, he will be in his forties. Now that's a long time!

Young men, once someone starts getting a criminal record, in some cases, the record and charges **NEVER, EVER** go away. That individual will always be in some computer system with their record attached to their name and a state-issued identification number. That same individual may even change their life, go on to apply to college, or fill out a job application and may be denied based solely on that record that shows delinquent criminal activity. **In some cases it's extremely hard for people with criminal records to obtain employment, go to school, apply for higher-level positions in companies, run for public office, receive state or national government positions, get a commercial driver licenses, and the list goes on and on.** Also, even if accepted into college, with some convictions, individuals are unable to obtain financial aid for school. Kickn' it with the "homies" may seem cool, but think about it, if you're in jail, the "homies" probably won't put money on your "books" and they will not be there for you when there is a prison riot. In most cases, they won't visit you in jail because they'll be too busy living their lives and having a good time. You may find out that all you have is yourself and possibly family members that may stand by you during an incarceration. However, the homies become scarce and you realize that loyalty isn't what you thought it was. The young man John, whose story I shared, is currently in a state prison outside of the state he was raised in. As a result, I'm sure that it is very hard for his family to visit him.

As mentioned in the stories above, no matter how small the negative things you may be doing are, they are the start of the **TRAP** being set. No one thinks that they're going to be the one to get caught, but **someone always does** because they "slipped up," or because the "homie" snitched on them. Believe me, people will talk when a deal can be made between their freedom and yours. Don't let this be you! Make good decisions, stay focused on your books, make good grades, surround yourself with positive people, get a mentor, and love yourself enough not to allow yourself to get caught in the "criminal activity traps."

Chapter 10
Take It to the House

"Be who God meant you to be and you will set the world on fire." – St. Catherine of Siena

You have so much potential! You have the potential to be an entrepreneur, an artist, an educator, a doctor, a lawyer, a senator, an engineer, or even the president; but it's time to move past just having potential. In science, there are two concepts: potential energy and kinetic energy. Potential energy is stored energy or energy at rest. For example, a car sitting with gasoline in the tank has potential energy. The car has potential to move, but it will not go anywhere until someone puts the key in the ignition, turns the car on, puts the car in drive, and presses the gas pedal. It's only after the car is in motion that it goes from having potential energy to having kinetic energy.

It's time for you to move past being a potentially good student, athlete, college student, honor student, musician, etc. and step in the area of having kinetic energy and putting your potential to work. It's time to **be** a great student, to **be** an honor roll student, **be** a great athlete, **be** a great college student, **be** a great musician, and to accomplish whatever your goals might be. In this book, we covered some of the obstacles that can hinder individuals from reaching their full potential. We discussed the importance of positive peer groups, being self-motivated, having a "Why," setting goals, persevering through difficult times, and the importance of decision-making. Many of you also completed the activities in the book and discovered if you're maximizing your twenty-four hours. You also learned if your friends have quality characteristics, and you wrote down your goals and steps to achieve them.

While many of the areas discussed in this book will help you get to the next level, they will not help you if, after reading this book and completing the activities, you use the book as a PlayStation stand or a place to sit your cups on top of. It's time to stop just being in a state of potential and hanging around people who do not have any positive, constructive business about themselves. It's time to stop quitting when things get a little difficult and doing things that don't help you get to the next level. I know you have the heart and desire to make your life a success. Continue to think positively, continue to stay hungry to achieve your goals, continue to use affirmations, and continue to keep your mind right. I want to end with lyrics from my version of the song " Background": " Instead of bars/Aim for stars/Don't know about you, but I am at Mars."

So what are you waiting for? Let's Get It!

Bonus Chapter 1

A Recipe for School Success

To be a successful student, there are a number of things you have to do: attend class, study, pay attention, stay away from negative influences, and the list goes on and on. It would take a great deal of time to explain every single thing, but what I will provide you with is a list of the most important details you must achieve to be successful. Coca-Cola would never share their recipe, but I'm going to share my recipe for student success.

1. **Go to class.** (So much of learning is absorbing what your teachers are telling you. You cannot expect to be successful when you're never present in class.)

2. **Be an active participant.** (Be an active participant in your learning; take notes, participate in group assignments, and ask questions when you do not understand something. Don't be a "bump on a log.") Ask questions!

3. **Get a planner.** (Write down your homework, due dates for assignments, study sessions, tutorial dates daily in each class, and check it daily so you're prepared.)

4. **Do your homework!** (We as educators don't give homework because we are evil creatures from another planet; we assign homework because it gives you a chance

to practice what we teach daily in the classroom. Great athletes don't just practice once a week, they practice daily or as often as possible. Homework is the same way. Great students don't just do homework once a week; they do it daily or as often as it's assigned. Lastly, homework allows teachers to see where their students are struggling. **As a teacher, I prefer for you to try to do the homework, even if you don't fully understand it, because then I know where to help you.**)

5. **Study something.** (If you don't have homework, study. There is always a test coming or a project due. Get a head start!)

6. **Make flash cards.** (Flash cards and graphic organizers may seem like a waste of time, **but they are not.** Create flash cards of key terms, concepts, and vocabulary. Study them daily. **You can sneak this in while riding the bus to school or after you eat breakfast in the cafeteria.**)

7. **Form study groups.** (Get with reliable classmates you'll actually study with. **Don't study with people you are going to talk to more than study with.**)

8. **Attend your teachers' tutorial sessions.** (All teachers have tutoring sessions. Attend them.)

9. **Complete all assignments.** (Turn in all assignments on time.)

10. **Use your resources.** (Everyone uses the Internet for all types of things, including Face book and YouTube. Use YouTube to watch videos on anything you're not

understanding in class. There are millions of videos on math, ELA, science, and social studies!)

11. **Be consistent!** (Set aside a specific time daily for studying and completing homework.)

Bonus Chapter 2

It's Time to Tolerate, Not Hate!
(Anti-Bullying)

In recent months, there has been much national attention on bullying. While the definition of bullying varies, there is a consensus that bullying is negative, hurtful, and cruel and something that should not occur. StopBullying.gov outlines several characteristics associated with bullying:

1. **Difference of power.** (Individuals being bullied have little power to "defend" themselves, and bullies generally have some form of power they use to hurt others.)

2. **Objective is to harm.** (The person doing the bullying is purposefully trying to hurt the other person.)

3. **Occurs often.** (Bullying occurs often and repeatedly to the same person.)

Bullying can take place in a number of forms, including verbally, socially, physically, and through cyber bullying. Verbal bullying occurs when individuals tease and say negative things to others. Social bullying occurs when people "spread negative rumors" with the purpose to hurt someone. Physical bullying occurs when the person in power physically hurts someone. Lastly, cyber bullying occurs when someone uses technology such as cell phones, computers, the Internet, and other technology to hurt someone.

Individuals who bully may have unresolved issues and have often been bullied themselves. As a result, they often bully others to feel good about themselves. Even so, with all the forms of bullying, there is one consistent aspect; there is a lack of respect and regard for the person being bullied. This lack of respect allows individuals doing the bullying to say and do cruel things without feeling bad about doing it. **Listen, having a lack of respect and disregard for others is very dangerous. We must remember that it was the lack of respect and tolerance that allowed slavery, the Holocaust, and the Apartheid to take place. Take note, you have the power to stop bullying!**

You can speak up against bullying by saying something as simple as *STOP!* You can also choose not to watch by walking away and telling an adult. This is very important because bullies like to have an audience and by walking away, you show your disapproval for what is occurring.

If you are being bullied, remember that it's not your fault. You are not alone and you have the right to be respected. Please tell someone like a teacher, school counselor, your parent, or your principal. You don't have to take being disrespected and hurt.

Bonus Chapter 3

Low Self-Esteem Trap

Many of the topics discussed above are issues that one can see with their eyes; however, low self-esteem is something that is not easily visible. Everyone has areas that he or she wishes they could improve in, like being a better speller or having more muscles. However, children with low self-esteem take their feelings of not being good enough to potentially dangerous levels. They feel they're "total failures," that they're not good at anything, and have feelings of hopelessness. People with low self-esteem respond in a number of ways including withdrawing, blaming themselves, and even hurting themselves. It is important to remember that we all have days where we feel a little down, but feeling negative about yourself should not be something you feel every day for long periods of time. If you have these negative feelings on an ongoing, consistent basis, you may need to reach out to someone for help. Seek help from your parents, school counselor, school social worker, principal, or any other adult that you trust. You are not "weak" or "lame" because you need help! I know many of us have been taught that we should be strong and handle our problems ourselves, but there are times when we all need help from others. Hey, if you ask me, it shows strength for someone to look for and accept help when it is needed.

To the parents and students reading this book, the middle school years can be very challenging because students are dealing with a number of pressures including creating an identity, body image, and trying to fit in. These normal processes can become even more difficult when a child has low self-esteem issues and poor self-concept. Parents and students, below are a few common characteristics of low self-esteem so that you can recognize the symptoms to help you or someone you know. (All characteristics of low self-esteem and poor self-concept aren't listed, so it's important to have dialogue in order to notice any signs that may be similar.)

1. Social withdrawal. (Not interacting with others much.)
2. Lack of social skills and confidence.
3. Not able to accept compliments.
4. Not able to judge yourself fairly.
5. Too much concern about what others think.
6. Not trusting your own opinion.

Parents and children, if you feel like you or someone you know is experiencing too many days of not feeling good about themselves, don't just ignore them and say that they will "get over it" or that they are "just having a bad day." There are times when outside help is needed. Help can be as simple as recommending that someone with low self-esteem talk to someone for help. If you yourself feel like you're having a difficult time, talk to an adult you trust about your concerns.

While these are not all the signs, they are useful in helping to recognize some of the indications of low self-esteem.

Before we can discuss ways to improve self-esteem, we must first get an understanding of some of the causes of low self-esteem. One cause of low self-esteem is constant criticism from people whose acceptance is important. These people include individuals like parents, family, peers, and teachers. Since these people's opinions matter so much, negative comments can be very hurtful and damaging to one's self-concept. Another cause of low self-esteem is the "inner critic," which is constant self-criticism. Over time the "inner voice" can be just as deadly as the criticism coming from others, because one can start to believe the negative things they say to themselves.

Another cause of low self-esteem, which we will discuss, is creating unrealistic expectations. Having expectations and/or goals that aren't reachable create a situation where you can never successfully complete them, which can lead to feelings of helplessness. So, what can we do to improve self-esteem? (Individuals whose low self-esteem is very consuming should seek assistance.) There are several things one can do. Let's see what they are:

1. Look at mistakes as something to learn from. (Remember that mistakes are part of learning and that we are constantly learning and growing.)
2. Understand that there are things you can and cannot change. (If you can change or improve something, then

start working on it. However, remember there are things that you cannot change, like eye color or how tall you are. With things that you cannot change, you have to learn to accept yourself just the way you are.)

3. Set good goals. (Determine what you want to achieve and create goals and steps that help you accomplish them. Don't set unrealistic goals or goals you aren't willing to work to complete.)

4. Understand that your opinion is valuable. (Everyone has a right to be heard. Don't let people silence your voice.)

5. Try new things. (Hey, you may discover that you're good at something you never knew you were.)

Remember, you are valuable, so never let anyone, even yourself, make you feel otherwise. In the words of Jo Blackwell-Preston, *"Don't you dare, for one more second, surround yourself with people who are not aware of the greatness that you are."*

3 Strikes and You're Out?

My mother told me of the history of her brother, who we will call Greg. Uncle Greg is someone I barely know because he was incarcerated starting as a youth in California's Youth Authority. It is sad to say that my uncle repeatedly made poor decisions that eventually resulted in him being incarcerated in county jail and prison before becoming one of California's "three strikers" in 1995. As a young man of twelve years old, I saw many sad days on my grandmother's face as the years passed while her son continued to serve out his **twenty-five-to-life (plus two years) sentence** that was handed down by a Long Beach judge. I know my grandmother did the best she could as a single parent raising eight children.

It's even sadder to say that my grandmother died two and a half years ago and her son, my uncle, could not even attend her funeral. Moving forward to a more positive note, my uncle Greg eventually spent the last fifteen years of his sentence availing himself of the many programs the prison system had to offer. This included the Restorative Justice Program (also called **reparative justice**), an approach to justice that focuses on the needs of the victims and the offenders, as well as the involved community.

The judge told Greg at the sentencing, "If I had a magic pill, I would give it to all the drug addicts that come through my court, but since I don't, I will sentence you to twenty-five years to life, plus two years." And so Greg's twenty-seven years was set. That was a harsh sentence for a nonviolent third strike, but the law was the law. Greg faced many challenges while in prison over the years. There were riots, stabbings, and he saw many inmates injured or die over the years from illness and death at the hands of another. But once Greg decided to make the *decision* to change, he sought redemption by facing his demons and by trying to restore what was left of his life. He began his road of redemption and has earned several certificates while incarcerated over the years. He has worked hard to change and redeem himself to soon become a productive and contributing member of society. Through his written correspondence to the family over the years, he appears to be a changed man. Many three-strike prisoners are getting a second chance in California since the recent passage of Prop. 36. My uncle is one of those three strikers that will go before the courts for resentencing and will be released soon.

The family is thankful and pleased for the amendment in the law, but isn't it sad that it took eighteen years in prison for my uncle to realize that he needed to make the **DECISION** to change. The price was not only paid by Greg. His sons, mother, brothers, sisters, and extended family also paid the price. What decisions will you make now, that will impact the rest of your life?

Letter to Young Men

Dear You,

You may not know it, but future generations are depending on you to move past just having potential and to live up to your potential. Yeah, I know, some of you may be living in one-parent households. I understand that some of you may have seen your parents only a few times. I'm aware that you may not have the things you want and that you're living in some pretty tough environments. Even so, there's no excuse to give up, to not put forth your best effort in school, to join gangs, to use drugs, or to participate in criminal activity.

Many of you may want to be rap artist because you've seen the music videos with rap artists driving Bugattis. You've watched music videos with artists who seem to be wearing the freshest gear, and you've seen artists with many attractive women in their videos. You've watched videos with artists that have large amounts of jewelry, but what you don't understand is that many of these artists' lives, videos, and tales of street life are a facade. Many of these artists rent cars and jewelry for their videos, pay girls to participate in their videos, and have never done many of the things they claim to do in their songs.

Many artists have had the truth surface about their lives and it turns out to be very inconsistent with what they have claimed in their lyrics. There are artists out there claiming to have been in the streets, "moved weight," and been shot or shot at others.

However, when you do the research, you find out they were in honors classes, went to school to be a nurse, were actually police officers, went to magnet schools, or came from two-parent households in the suburbs. The music industry is a business, and artists will sell you any dream to get an album sold.

So many young men are making decisions that will lead to jail, getting injured or death while trying to imitate what they see in videos and TV. Don't believe the hype! There are other avenues to be successful other than being a rapper, a professional athlete, or being out in the streets. You have the ability to do whatever it is you want. It does not matter where you live or if you are from a single-parent household. It doesn't matter how much they hate on you or if no one in your family graduated college. The key is you! You just have to make up your mind that you are going to be different. You can be the first high school or college graduate in your family and you can break the cycle of gang involvement. So, what is it going to be? Mr. Phillips is rocking with you. Let's get it!

Sincerely,
Patrick Phillips

Letter to Parents

Dear Parents,

I know how hard you work to give your children a better life than you had. I know the overtime hours you put in, the side jobs you take to make a little extra money, and how you sacrifice personally so that your children can have what they need. In more than a decade of working with children and families, I rarely encountered parents who didn't want the best for their children. However, at times, parents do make slight errors in judgment that hinder the development of their children.

This world can be a cruel place, and if we don't adequately prepare our young men for the real world, they will struggle significantly. In this letter I want to discuss several things, but first I want you to understand that my goal is not to be offensive, but rather thought-provoking.

As an educator and social worker, I've witnessed parents make excuses for their young man's shortcomings—excuses for poor grades, sagging pants, negative attitude, and disrespectful behavior. I've heard comments like, "Well his father isn't around...he's just a little headstrong...why not judge him for who he is and not what he wears...why are you grading him so tough..." In addition, parents sometimes reward negative behavior and may not even know it. I can't tell you the number of times I've seen students get suspended and return to school with $170 shoes, or they receive a call home regarding poor behavior and the next day return with a forty-dollar haircut, or they do not complete chores, but continue to get seventy-five-dollar jeans and shirts.

When this type of behavior occurs, young men are being taught that they don't have to be accountable and will still be rewarded, which is far from what happens in the real world.

I want to share an experience with you. When I was in middle school, I started becoming very talkative in class and started slacking on my schoolwork. I came home with a bad report card and my mother let me have it. She took all my shoes and clothes and bought me two school uniforms with bowties. She also sat in all my classes for two days! This was such a tough punishment because not only was I wearing a school uniform while everyone else was not, but it was tough because I was attending school in South Central, Los Angeles, aka "the hood!" LOL! My mom knew what she was doing. I remember that punishment to this day, even though it occurred nearly twenty years ago. My mother never made excuses for me and always held me accountable and to a high standard, which is what we must do for our young men if they're to be successful.

The second aspect that I feel is very important to address is the occurrence of parents saying, "I don't know what to do with him," referring to their young men being allowed to do whatever they like as children. I cannot tell you how many parents have said this to me referring to their sons. Parents, you cannot let your young men run uninhibited with no boundaries as a young child and then, when he's in middle and high school, wonder why you have no control over their behavior. Intervene early because believe me, it's much better if you get him now versus watching the authorities get him later. Hey, I know your struggles, and I'm with you. Let's make future generations of young men who are strong and great contributors to society. We can do it together!

Sincerely,

Patrick Phillips

Thank You

Thank you for your purchase and allowing me to share my perspective of what it takes to avoid some of life's traps and get to the next level. I say throughout the book that you have the ability to accomplish your goals, overcome your challenges, and make your life a success. I was once where many of you are, wondering how I would be successful and wondering how I was going to get out the hood. I'm not going to lie; at times it won't be easy. You have to get up every day and fight for a better future for yourself by pursuing your education and making good solid decisions.

There are plenty of people in this world that will give up on you; don't **you** be one of those people. Get up every day and grind. Get up every day with a purpose. Get up every day and prove people wrong! Get up every day and push to make your life a success.

Patrick Phillips, MSW

INFORMATION LINKS

- Change Factor

  http://www.mrphillipsthechangeagent.com/#!change-factor-/c1v03

- Music For Change

  http://www.mrphillipsthechangeagent.com/#!multimedia/c1ml9

DISCLAIMER FOR WEB LINKS:

The website links below are provided for informational purposes only and do not constitute endorsement of any products or services provided. Links are subject to change, expire, or be redirected without any notice.

- http://www.stopbullying.gov

- http://www.stopcyberbullying.org/index2.html

- http://www.ncpc.org/newsroom/current-campaigns/bully-prevention

- http://www.cdc.gov/alcohol/fact-sheets/underage-drinking.htm

- http://findyouthinfo.gov/youth-topics/preventing-youth-violence

BOOK SPECIFICS

Cover Art: Maurel Denge

Graphic Design: Creative Notions Design Group

Editing: MNG

Booking Information

Mr. Phillips The Change Agent

info@mrphillipsthechangeagent.com

Order Information

If you would like to order additional books, CDs, or other merchandise by this author, please place orders online at:

www.MrPhillipsTheChangeAgent.com

ABOUT THE AUTHOR

Patrick Phillips is an educator, social worker, mentor, songwriter, empowerment speaker, and educational consultant. He is a self-proclaimed change agent, as he works to empower individuals to move past potential into the realm self-efficacy and self-actualization. He is often reminding youth and adults that "your present circumstances or environment do not define you or dictate your outcome unless you allow them to."

He has been instrumental in getting students to look at standardized testing positively by creating positive songs that influence youth. Many educators have shared his songs with their students to help reduce test anxiety and encourage effective test-taking skills.

Raised in a single-parent household in Los Angeles, California, Mr. Phillips witnessed the negative consequences that poverty, limited opportunity, and gang violence can have on youth, young adults, and families. Mr. Phillips decided that rather than be a statistic, he would use his experiences to help individuals realize they can overcome their obstacles. He continues to facilitate empowerment lectures to inspire individuals for positive change one organization and school at a time.

He lives in Atlanta, Georgia, with his wife and son.

"Your current circumstance does not dictate your future outcome".

-Patrick Phillips

Notes

Notes

Notes

Notes

Notes

Made in the USA
Monee, IL
15 November 2021